COLLATERAL DAMAGE:

VICTIMLESS CHILDREN OF MY DIVORCE

BY ROY GARDNER

RoseDog Books
PITTSBURGH, PENNSYLVANIA 15238

RoseDog Books
585 Alpha Drive, Suite 103
Pittsburgh, PA 15238
Visit our website at www.rosedogbookstore.com

ISBN: 979-8-89211-121-8
eISBN: 979-8-89211-619-0

CONTENTS

INTRODUCTION

A PROUD DAD 1974

It seems like just yesterday, when I was sitting on the front porch of my apartment in the North side of Corpus Christi, Texas, wondering where my next meal would come from. Was it going to be powdered eggs, butter sandwich or nothing?

When would I have to lie to the bill collectors again, and tell them my mother was not home, because she didn't have the money to pay a bill that day?

I lived with my mom and older brother Freddie and we were on Welfare. My life was the same as everyone else around me.

The future didn't look promising, most people were on drugs, homeless and unemployed. My mom was a single parent constantly looking for work.

The few people that did make it out were football or basketball players with tremendous talent. My talent level was nonexistent. I didn't play sports in high school.

If someone would have told me that I would accomplish the things that I have, I would have laugh at them. My only thoughts growing up was to make it to the next day.

A close friend who ran the recreation center did tell me once that I would never do anything good with my life. I think I made her job more difficult with my attitude and stubbornness.

Now when I see her she is in awe that I really made something of myself. I think that her words may have played an important part in my success. I have never told her that but the next time I see her, I will.

This book is intended to show that in many cases, no matter what you do to show your kids that you are there for them, it want matter if the other party has done irreversible/collateral damage over a long period of time. This is exactly what happen to me as it relates to my relationship with my three kids.

I have been accused and judged to be a bad parent by my two oldest because I refused to go to battle with their mom over the years, after we divorced. I refused to fight around them.

I thought that I was doing the right thing for my kids because of what was happening in my marriage and after the divorce, and how this would have such a negative impact on them. I didn't want them to witness the drama and grow to resent me.

The short time they still lived in the same city as I did, my attempted visitations did not go smoothly. I then realized that my divorce would take the same bumpy road as most.

My profession as a police officer took me to many homes of parents that argued, fought in front of the kids and even killed. I made up my mind early on that my kids would never experience that, at least not from me.

It became more difficult to be a part of their lives when they moved out of the city. This was at a time when there were no cell phones, internet or facetime.

As with many divorced parents I relied on the other parent, because of their ages, to allow them to call me, but that didn't happen for a long time.

I had no input into who would have full custody, the judge made that decision. I had no say about them relocating, their mom made that one. I had no say so about other people living in their house with them. Could this have played a part in what was to come? I really don't know, unlike many separated or divorced parents I never once interrogated them about who their mom was dating or living with. Maybe I should have.

I thought I had a healthy relationship with all three of them only to find out 40 years later that two of them never got over the divorce, because of what they were told.

Because of the false information and lies that they were told, they are angry and bitter, only at the wrong person.

They thought for reasons unknown to me that I had moved on with another marriage and child and forgotten about them. Where this came from, I think most of us have the answer. It is very common in many divorces.

So I am asking anyone who reads this book, no matter whether you have custody or not, to think long and hard about what you tell your kids about the other parent.

Not everyone is mentally able to balance their emotions, especially if they are given the wrong information as to what is going on and at an early age.

After my divorce I worked long and hard to provide for my kids. I wasn't in the house so I have no idea where the money went. I was not one of those people who tried to control what the money was spent on. I trusted that the mom would use the funds to feed and clothes my kids.

I recently received some disturbing information about their living conditions as children. I refuse to say what it is, because it's in the past. It does shine light on why these things happen.

I wished I could say that I trusted that she would reassure my kids that although I wasn't there on a daily bases, that I was still their loving and caring father, but I knew this was not happening.

I even voluntarily increased the amount of money that the courts ordered me to pay for child support. This was the only way in the beginning, before they moved that I could come around to visit them without the drama.

I also did it because I knew that it would be difficult to provide all the things that they needed on what I was ordered to pay.

I paid child support for more than 15 years and never was late once or missed a payment, but I guess it still wasn't enough. I assumed that the money was being used in a productive way, but now I know differently.

I answered every bell when they called me needing something, I never said no when they were kids and seldom said no as adults, especially if it had to do with my grandkids.

So for all you parents out there feeling like you failed your kids, you didn't. If you did what you could, the best you could, then you are not bad parents.

Sometimes it just a bad marriage or relationship with the wrong person that is more damaging to your relationship with the kids than anything else.

Your kids are going to have to grow mentally and understand how life goes. If they are weak minded, selfish or spoiled then they want ever understand.

We are only here for one life and you need to make the most of it. You only get one mom and one dad, once they are gone, that's it.

It's funny how kids sometimes complain that their parent favors one child over another. They never stop to consider in cases of divorce, how they may be favoring one parent over the other.

I really thought that once they became adults and started dating, that they would grow to understand that these things happen.

I made tremendous amount of trips to see them over the years that appear to have been in vain. I thought we were in a good place but it appears that the wounds are too deep.

In this book I will not mention the two oldest by their names for privacy reasons. I will refer to them by their first initial.

My concern now is the grandkids, there is a chapter that addresses this.

As you read on, you may not agree with some of the things in the book, but this is my life and experience with my kids.

In Memory Of

Zane Keith Gardner

I would like to dedicate this book to my youngest son Zane, who is not with me today but forever in my heart. He was the victim of a terrible crime that hunts me every day. I am sure his mother, who is not the focus of this book feels even worse, being he was her only child.

After losing a child in such a way, it is hard to cope with the ones who are still here and unappreciated of my love for them

Chapter One

‿‿

My name is Roy Gardner, I am in my 70's and I have lived in South Texas my entire life. I attended a segregated school name Solomon Coles in Corpus Christi, Texas and graduated in 1968. I graduated from Roy Miller High School after Coles was closed due to segregation.

I was born somewhere in Houston, Texas in 1950. I was told in the 5th Ward. My mom was a single parent with three sons. We left there at an early age and we moved to corpus. At one point my mom sent me to stay with my aunt in corpus for reasons I don't know, I am sure it had to do with trying to provide for three kids with no job and no money.

My aunt, which we called Aunt Nell had a home in corpus and was a single lady with no kids. She wanted kids and I guess when the opportunity came to care for me, she jumped on it.

Aunt Nell was my mom half-sister. My mother's maiden name was Collier. She had several brother and sisters. In Corpus there was her brothers Isaac Collier and Bob Collier. We also had an Aunt Rose in La Yola California, who we thought was rich because she would fly to Corpus on a regular bases and give us money. She had another sister name Lucinda Ellison in San Antonio.

Aunt Rose had no kids but Bob had at least two sons, Percy and Zeke. Lucinda had two Sons who names I don't recall.

I am including these family members in the event my grandkids want to research the family tree. All of the aunts and uncles I spoke about are on my mother's side of the family and they are all deceased.

Again, I know nothing of my father's side of the family.

We also had an uncle name Daisy Dukes who owned a ranch in Lulling Texas. I do recall that we would visit his ranch and ride horses in the summer. Aunt Nell last name was also Dukes.

The ranch had an oil well on it and all of the family members received monies for most of their lives until the land was foreclosed on in2020 when the taxes were not paid.

This was devastating for me because of the large amount of land as well as the drilling that was still going on. This land had been in the family for many years. This is what occurs when a family is not united and communication with each other.

Once my mom was ready to leave Houston, I am guessing that she may have been getting away from a bad relationship with my dad who was from Houston, she called my aunt to drive her to corpus. On the way to Corpus my mom and aunt got into a custody fight over me. I think I was living with my aunt and my mom wanted me back. Somehow I bumped my head on the hood of the car and don't recall what happen after that.

I have had a number of head injuries caused by swings, swimming and other injuries which have affected parts of my childhood and long term memory.

Things worked themselves out and I and my brother Fred and my mom lived with my aunt until my mom was able to get her own apartment.

That apartment was in government housing at 1910 Tuskegee. It was a block from the Corpus Christi Police department. This was the highest crime rate community in the city. It was a predominant black community. This is where I lived for most of my childhood.

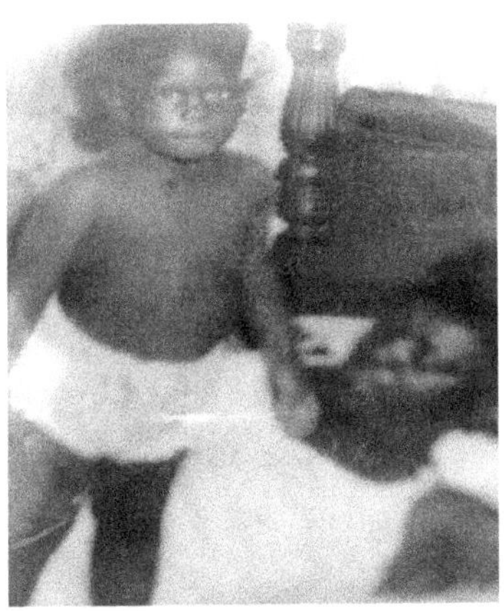

My mom got a job working at a cleaners to support us, my older brother Joe, stayed in Houston. He had a different dad and was 15 years older than Fred and I.

My mom was strict, she insisted that we do our part in cleaning the house and ironing our school clothes. She didn't hesitate punishing us for all of the mischief we got into, and we got into a lot. She didn't tolerate cursing, smoking or drinking.

Her discipline usually involve an extension cord or tree branch. She would make us go and get the tree limb and if it was not big enough then she would find one bigger. We usually had to strip down to our briefs and you know the rest.

We had the typical projects life, football in the street, swimming at the local YMCA. Lots of basketball in parks with no nets and under inflated balls. Track meets in the streets. Hot summers with no air conditioning and government food.

As you can imagine, crime was very high in the projects. The community which was called Leathers Projects was known as 'The cuts'.

This was because of the number of cuttings that occurred on a regular bases. It was interesting that it was called the cuts, I guess most people in the community couldn't afford to buy guns, so they carried knives.

The police was not someone that we trusted. Usually when we got in trouble and was being chased by the police, we had designated routes to run where clothes lines had been lowered to slow the police down, as we ducked to avoid them.

The clothes lines were string not wire and I don't recall any police officers getting hurt from them.

Because we had little money we didn't eat out much, occasionally on my mom's payday we were able to go to the local hamburger stand, called the Bigger Burger Stand, and get a burger.

The second most memorable treat was the "Moon Cookies". They were two cookies for a penny. We would buy ten cents worth, 20 cookies, and break them up in a brown paper bag. This would give us a bag full of cookies to eat on for the rest of the day.

As I got older I wished for some of the finer things in life like new clothes instead of hand me downs from friends and family. I don't know how but I think it was peer pressure, I started going downtown to the fancy clothing store and doing some shopping. I would steal, yes steal clothing. I had what I thought was the perfect scheme. I would take several pair of pants or shirts into the dressing room and put them on under my clothing and walk out without paying.

I am still in awe that I never got caught, which was not a good thing as you will read later on.

When I became a teenager and old enough to work in the cotton fields in the summer months, I did. A truck would come by around 5am. and honk its horn. We would grab our sacks, no lunch, no hats no shades and no water, and get aboard. They would drive to a cotton field and we would pull cotton from sunup to sundown. It would pay by the pound but when I started I was only able to use a small Croker sack which only held a small amount of cotton. As the years went by I got to where I was able to carry a 10 foot sack and fill it with 200 pounds of cotton. I felt like I had arrived and was ready to take on the world.

The method used back then was to walk a good distance from the truck into the field and start picking (pulling) from there back toward the truck, this way as the sack got heavier to drag, you got closer to the truck. Once you reached the truck to weight your sack, you had to be able to lift it onto the scale.

Needless to say it was extremely hot. The trucks had food and drinks that you could purchase on credit until you got paid at the end of the week when your weekly total was added up. I don't recall how much we got per pound. Once they deducted what you owed for drinks, food, gloves and stuff, you earnings was not really worth the labor but it was the only way of making good, honest money at the time.

As I got older I worked a number of jobs, from dishwashing, shining shoes, Coke a Cola bottling company on the assembly line which was very dangerous when the bottles would stack up on the convey belt and start to fall off onto the cement floor and shatter all around us.

The most difficult job was one where a close friend of mine now works. It was called Sam Kane Meat Company back then but the name have changed. They would slaughter the cows and skin them for the meat. The hides would then be stacked in a pit the size of a swimming pool. Salt was scattered on them to keep the smell contained or preserve the hides, not sure which. Our job was to get into the pit and stack the hides onto the pallets by hand. At the end of the day you were not able to get all of the stench off of you. On the ride home your friends could smell the truck coming from blocks away.

I mentioned my older brother in Houston, he was a fighter. By that I meant that we were told that he spent time in the army and did some boxing. He also did a lot of drinking, as a result he would get into fights both in Houston and Corpus that ended in serious bodily injuries, to either him or someone else.

One night while Fred and I was sitting on the porch trying to keep cool because we had no air conditioning, my older brother stumbled up to us. He was bleeding from the abdomen, he had been stabbed. He asked us to drive him to Houston, which even today I found that request to be humorous, aside from his injury, because not only did we not have a driver's license or know how to drive, our family didn't own a car.

Believe it or not, this community which once hosted such people as James Brown and other celebrities, no longer exist. In the last couple of years the city decided to demolish the entire community and make room for a new bridge and business area. The majority of people who have lived there all of their lives have been relocated throughout the city.

It is very hard to even drive through the area and see what it looks like now.

The police station in the area was relocated many years ago.

CHAPTER TWO

❦

BROTHERS

I just spoke about my oldest brother Joe. He went by several names, Joe McCain, Willie Lee McCain and Joe Gardner.

I think these different names came in handy when being stopped or arrested by the police.

He went on to live a very unproductive life, which was typical for many unemployed, uneducated people at that time, in his situation. He never married, didn't own a home, and never had kids. He lived on the streets most of his life and suffered from alcoholism and seizures.

At one point I took him off the streets and was able to get him into an apartment. This didn't last long because he lived alone and would have seizures causing his to fall and injure himself.

I had to eventually place him in a home for his own safety. He soon came down with lung cancer and passed away at an early age.

I wanted to give him a military funeral but when I tried to confirm his service in the military, I was unable to do so.

I had to settle for an ordinary funeral. It made me questions all of the things I was told about him.

To my knowledge he never had a steady job, he moved around a lot from city to city.

As I look back I question how he survived before becoming ill. I think like many of the men in my family, he depended on a woman to give him a place to live and food to eat.

To my knowledge he didn't graduate from high school, not sure how far he got.

He was a good looking man and fit, so finding a woman to take him in was easy back then. The bar was not high at all.

He was not a provider but a protector.

Fred

He was a year older than me. We lived in the same home most of our lives. He was drafted into the army as a cook and served two years. I too was drafted two years later into the army.

We both were sent to Germany for two years.

He had several skills such as barber and cooking, which he learned in the army.

Fred was laid back, easy going and non-confrontational. He has two kids, worked several jobs over the years but decided that he wanted to sell drugs, marijuana.

Because of his low key personality he was given the nickname of (Koolie).

He became a dealer at the same time I started a career in law enforcement, to be covered in a later chapter.

Needless to say this made my job as a police officer more challenging. People in the neighborhood just assumed that I was either a crooked cop or I just turned my head the other way to allow Fred to deal drugs.

Neither of these were true, Fred respected my position and never put me in any compromising positions. I thank him for that.

He unfortunately was arrested a lot for selling drugs and spent many years in prison. This took him away from his kids in a different way than my situation.

This was when I visited Fred in prison.

We were always close in spirit and had a special bond. Like myself (old school) we just understood each other. We didn't have to hug, shake hands or say "I Love You". This was not something you did growing up on the streets. This would later come back to haunt me with my relationship with my kids.

Once Fred stop dealing drugs as he got older our relationship got even stronger. He continued to live in the same neighborhood that we grew up in. I would visit him on a weekly bases.

He became ill and was unable to work. He started drinking heavily which contributed to his medical problems.

His kids unlike mine would come and visit him on a regular bases. I can count the number of times my kids visited me on one hand over the past 20 years.

He had no money to give them but they came anyway, he was their dad. His kids, like him, was raised on the streets, mine was not. They appreciated having a dad, they knew how rare that it was in the black community where most families have a single parent, usually just a mom.

They never to my knowledge, held it against him, for going to prison most of their lives, instead they enjoyed him when he was there. They would come by and play dominoes, bring him food or just visit and drink with him.

I can honestly say that I never once heard his kids talk back to him or disrespect him in any way. They loved their dad for who he was and not what he was, an absentee dad because of prison.

I always felt bad for his kids. They never lived with him. He was never able to provide much for them or their mother. His son followed in his footsteps and experience some of the hard aches that Fred did. He has since gotten himself together. His daughter, I don't see that often.

I always wondered if the roles were reversed and I lived Fred life with my kids, how they would judge me as a parent. If they had to endure the life that his kids lived, would they have survived?

If they are bitter at me now, then they would surly hate me if they had his kid's life.

I look at Fred the way I look at my mom. He did the best he knew how. It's hard not to give in to peer pressure growing up in the projects and wanting more in life. I saw many of my friends take that same path which was laced with money and jewelry in the beginning, heart aches and prison time in the end.

My kids and his try to keep in touch as far as I know. Mostly on social media.

I always looked up to Fred although I never told him so. He was my last surviving sibling. My last family member in Corpus other than some distant cousins. The last person I knew that I could lean on.

He didn't go to college, didn't have a car or bank account in the end. He didn't have a career or even a home but he was my mother's child. I shit you not, he was a very caring, loving person. This is how we were raised and why I give my mother so much credit. She set the bar and I wish the mother of my kids would have done the same. I truly would not be writing this book, but rather hanging with my grandkids, which I miss dearly.

Can you imagine if my mom would have spoken often about my dad, the things she might had told us. I am sure back then he laid hands on her, he didn't provide for us and we NEVER saw him.

I can only imagine the hate we might have had toward him, thus making us angry adults in life.

It hurts and I never tried to show it but to have never spent the night at any of my three kid's homes, on the many trips there.

Part of it was that a few times I was not alone and didn't want to chance any drama. It is also true that I like my privacy but it's the lack of an invite that stings.

Fred past several years later but his memory lives on, he was my big brother, he looked out for me.

That's something that over the years I find lacking from my kids, they all live in the same city, yet they don't spend much time together.

They are not there for each other when hard times pay a visit. I have to watch my youngest daughter deal with some serious issues by herself.

I think this is another example of what they didn't learn as children. If you are not there to help each other when times are bad, who will?

I can truly say that I would have taken a bullet for Fred.

This will surely ruffle some feathers but from what I have seen over the years and what I am told each time I ask one about the other, it is more fact than fiction.

Chapter Three

Disasters

During my youth there were several things that shaped my life. Once I graduated from high school I attended a college nearby. I was able to do this by using VA benefits that my dad, that I never knew, had earned. I have no recollections, pictures, knowledge or anything about my dad. My mom never talked about him. She was from the school that says, if you don't have anything good to say then don't say anything.

We were only told that our dad who had the same name as Fred (Freddie Lee Gardner) was from Houston and was killed when he was struck by a train.

You may find it odd, but neither Fred nor I spent time trying to know about our dad. We focused mostly on staying alive, day to day. Even today with all the DNA, computer searches and things, I have not had the desire to research him. The reason is that I don't expect to find that he accomplished much in his life. Not that he couldn't but based on the resources or lack of available to him and people like my mom and the hard times with no formal education and rampant discrimination.

My focus has been to set a good example for my kids and hope that they don't have to experience what I have, it's a different world now. It's not perfect but there are opportunities that didn't exist in the 50's and 60's.

Anyway, while home my first semester from college I was driving across some railroad tracks in my car when I was struck by a train. Believe it or not, today is the first time I realize the weird connection with my dad and I as far as trains.

Luckily, I was not injured but my car was totaled which made it impossible to go back to school. Because I was not in school and there was a draft for soldiers, I got drafted into the army. This was one of the scariest times in my life, because of the Vietnam War.

Prior to going into the service I got married. This would turn out to be the mother of my three oldest children.

After completing all my training in Louisiana and Georgia, I was shipped off to Germany. This is where the cover photograph was taken back in 1971. I had never been out of the state of Texas.

The training was tough. The focus then was on sending soldiers to Vietnam to fight. There were soldiers that got stationed in other locations such as the US.

The military decided to make me a Military Police Officer in spite of my tendency to get into trouble. The assignment was a result of my high test results. This is when I learned my first valuable lesson.

I lived off base and was driving a VW that I purchased for $50. I spray painted it with several cans of blue paint. It served as my transportation until I was discharged. I remember selling it for $50 when I left Germany. It had no brakes and I had to sometimes use my feet with the door open to stop.

One night when I was getting off of patrol duty I found myself short of gas to get home. I lived off base because the mother of my children was there as well.

My patrol partner had the perfect solution. We were patrol officers in a government car and routinely filled up our work vehicle at the gas pumps on base. He suggested that when we gas up the police unit, I could get gas for my car and no one would notice, mainly because it was late at night and no one was around. I followed him to the pumps and once he finished pumping gas into the police car, I pulled my car up to the same pump, placed the nuzzle into my tank and as I got ready to pump the gas, my sergeant, whom we got the gas key from earlier, drove by us. He didn't stop, he didn't speak and he just left. I realized that I was in serious trouble so I decided not get any gas.

Nothing was said or done about that night until months later when a Special Military Investigator was sent to our base to investigate the theft of hundreds of gallons of military gas from our base. Apparently someone had been putting gas in a tanker truck and selling it.

I knew at that time my military service was over as well as my life. I tried to convince them without proof that I didn't take any gas that night or any other time. My prayers were answered and I was not disciplined. Several people who was involved in the thefts were either court martialed, dishonorably discharged or incarcerated. I went on to complete my military obligation, promoted to Spec 4, and learned a valuable lesson from this mistake. I was reassigned to my hometown base a few months before being discharged because I was going to be a dad, every man's dream.

Back in the States, or as it was called then, "The World", I became a father, with no job. I knew then that it was time to step up and become a man. One that would make my mother, wife and especially baby girl proud.

I was in for a big surprise, the responsibilities that came with being a father and husband with no money, no degree or work experience. The challenges of marriage in your early 20's, living in the Ghetto. I needed a way out no matter what.

I was not very athletic and didn't play sports in high school.

Chapter Four

⌘

Career

I thought they would be proud:

Once I returned to the States after serving my country, I found that nothing had changed. The jobs were scarce, the streets were more violent and dangerous and drugs were everywhere.

I had a child on the way and I knew that I had to find a good job in order to provide for my family.

I had little or no work experience other than my military experience. The army had decided that I was best suited to be a Military Police officer which is what I did for the two years I served. For some reason it never crossed my mind to reenlist, probably because I didn't want to join in the first place. Like most 20 year olds in the 70's I was scared by the war in Vietnam. If I had it to do over I would proudly serve and probably with the marine corp. I served alongside many marines and came to respect their wiliness to fight for their country no matter what.

I wish I could remember the person who suggested that I try the police department. The police station was two blocks from my home. We had walked by the building for years and saw the inmates screaming out the windows.

While I was away in the army a young police officer had been killed walking out the back door of the police station to get into his police car. As I said, the station was located in the black community and tension between the police and that community had always been bad, well it was taken to another level, which is what I was told, when the officer got killed and the suspect got arrested. It was all hands on deck looking for the person who shot the officer. He was identified and arrested and since been released from prison.

No one in the community wanted to be a cop. I myself didn't have a desire to be one but I found myself applying for my family.

The pay was low but the academy I tested for was offering college courses to the police cadets for the first time, as well as the regular salary. By me being a veteran I was able to take advantage of this opportunity, so I joined.

My intentions was to spend four months in the academy and collect the money and then quit. Curiosity took over after graduation and I decided to wait and see what being a cop was about. While stationed in Germany as a MP (Military Police) I got a taste of it. It had its perks but didn't motivate me to be one.

Most of the MP's wanted to return home and do this type of work, it didn't excite me. One of the reasons was because I had two minor encounter with police officers.

One was when hurricane Celia struck Corpus and destroyed the city. Needless to say my home was not damaged but I was able to get some items from the Red Cross. As I was walking home with the items a police officer who I had encounter once before, knew me, knew where I lived and knew that my home was not heavily damaged, just a few broken windows.

When he saw me with the items he made me take them back. He had also made contact with me on a minor call involving my car being in the shop and me not being able to claim it.

These two contacts were not serious but didn't leave a good impression on me. Looking back the officer was actually friendly and professional in his approach.

Once I graduated from the academy and had a job to support my family, I was on my way to better times. I didn't think about quitting because I didn't have another job waiting for me. I found that the pay would get better once I went on patrol. I also learned that there were other opportunities to increase my income by working off duty jobs such as parties, dances and security.

I want talk much about my police career, only as it relates to my family and kids. I will say that the long days and hours of working to support the family, gave us a better life but took its toll on the marriage. I was the man in the relationship and at that time the man of the house was expected to be the sole provider.

I can honestly say that if I was given a choice, I would not hesitate to do it again. I really came to love and respect the profession.

But I must say that it has changed a lot in the past few years since I retired. The number of police shootings, officers killed or sent to prison, would make most people think twice.

I also felt that I was giving back to the community that I grew up in, even though the people I served in that community felt differently. There were many that did appreciate the police presence and protection we provided.

I had a very long and rewarding career which help make me the man I am today.

I believe that I open the door for more local African Americans in the city to want to be police officers. Several people that I grew up with later joined the force.

As life went on I became the father of three kids, two daughters and a son. As I stated earlier the police pay was not that good. In order to provide a comfortable life for my family I had to take on server side jobs.

My wife didn't work, she was a stay home wife with the three small kids.

I found myself working four to five jobs at one time. I was a police officer, I continued going to college to draw benefits, I worked as the security guard at the apartments we lived in, in exchange for free rent and I worked weekly at a local food store providing security. I would also work any other security jobs that were available such as football or basketball game, dances etc.

We were able to live a comfortable life but now I realize how much it took me away from my family. Sometimes when you think you are right, you could be wrong.

My marriage started to suffer, and before any on my kids reached the age of 10, I was divorced. This had little to do with my work, but something out of my control.

We went to court and worked out the child support and child custody agreements. The contacts we had after the divorce were not good, especially for the kids to witness. As a result I didn't visit as often as I wanted to. I wasn't able to talk to them since they were too young to call. I had to settle with seeing them whenever I could.

I later remarried and had a second son. This is when I think things really took a turn for the worse.

They were of the impression that I had another family and had moved on and forgotten about them. I was not aware of this for some time.

If that wasn't bad enough, they soon moved from Corpus to Austin, four hours away.

Over the years I made frequent trips to see them. I thought I was spending quality time with them.

On a few occasions they were in town and I was able to visit but for the most part I had to find their location and go see them as oppose to them being dropped off at my home.

My tenth Year on the force and after being promoted to Lieutenant I was scheduled to work that day when I learned that my two girls were in town. They were visiting their mom's friend with no plans of visiting me. I told them I would come by once I checked in for work. I drove to their location in the police car to see them for a short visit. The house was fenced in with a pad lock on the gate. They came out to see me, we talked briefly between a hurricane fence that separated us. There was a small child climbing over the fence to my side. Once he made it to my side of the fence he placed his finger in my gun holster and pulled the trigger on my gun. The holsters at that time were not equipped with the safety devices that are now used.

The gun went off striking me in the upper leg. No one else was injured. I am sure my girls were scared hearing the gun shot and seeing their dad bleeding.

I was rushed to the hospital to be treated. I was fortunate that the bullet passed down my thigh instead of into my leg. I waited to hear from my girls hoping that they were not traumatized. To my surprise I never heard from them. They never called or came to the hospital. I was there for several days. Luckily the bullet didn't inter my leg but I needed a skin graph. They didn't know the extent of my injuries so I thought for sure their mom would drive them there. I found out later that they had went back to Austin and as I mentioned, never called to check up on me or call, neither did my son.

I don't recall their ages but I had been on for ten years, my oldest was born before I joined, which would had made her around 10. My youngest was probably 5 or 6.

I told myself over the years that I was not angry but I knew I was lying to myself. I didn't want them to feel bad. But when the finger pointing started about my short comings as a dad, I would remind myself and them on occasions of that day.

I know that I am dancing around the elephant in the room, I have with them for many years. I still try to avoid any confrontations, but any reasonable person knows whose responsibility it was, that day, to see to it that my girls come to the hospital and be with me before going back to Austin.

This should serve as a reference to what was being taught to them in their house hold about me.

My youngest son became handicap and this devastated my wife and me. It turned our life upside down. The uncertainty of him living or dying, being hospitalized for long periods of time and eventually being homebound was beyond stressful.

My wife, the mother dedicated her life to our son's every need, until he passed.

I don't recall much about those years and my relationship with my other kids. This is something that no one wants to have to go through. I didn't expect my kids to understand what it was like. I hope that they will never go through something like this with their kids.

I am sure I spent less time with the other kids because we were not able to travel with him. His illness lasted years and eventually he passed from the injuries.

As when I got shot in the leg and my kids weren't there for comfort or support, they never came to corpus to visit their brother Zane during his many hospital stays in the hospital. These are the kids that are trying to label me as a bad, uncaring dad.

My wife at the time and I was ill equipped to deal with his long term medical condition and even less prepared to handle his passing.

These were very difficult times and that even today I have not recovered from. The loss of a child stays with you for the rest of your life and it doesn't get easier with time.

As with many similar cases, this contributed to me and my second wife getting divorced. We probably should have gotten some counseling but we didn't.

Discrimination:

This is always a tough topic to talk about. The truth is that unless you have been a victim of discrimination, you really don't know how it feels and what it does to you mentally.

I am not one who uses the race card at all. I accept that there are people out there that are prejudice and that will never change.

Prejudice in the 60's and 70's was totally different than it is now.

By looking at the cover and pictures in this book, you know that I am African American, I prefer being called Black.

My earliest encounter of discrimination was when I was stationed in Germany. I had brought my wife over and was in need of housing. I called around and found an apartment for rent. After talking to the owner I drove to the location only to be told that it was no longer available.

I felt without proof that once she saw that I was black, she decided not to rent to me.

Fast forward 50 years and after retiring from the police department I was hire by a friend who was the chief of police in Uvalde Texas. This was around 2010. We had worked together for many years at CCPD.

I traveled there from Corpus, met the city manager and his staff and agreed to take the job. I returned home and started looking for housing in Uvalde. I located an ideal piece of property for rent, contacted the seller and agreed to a contract. When I went back to see the property and pay the rent, I was told that they had rented it to someone that they thought was me, I didn't buy it. Uvalde at that time had very few blacks living there.

Needless to say that I encountered my share of discrimination on the job as a police officer, both from within the department and in the field. This was something I expected and I was ready to deal with it. Far too many incidents to talk about in this book.

To give you an idea of what the police force was like when I joined, the black officers who came before me were not allowed to ride in a police car. They were assigned in the north side of town only (black community) as a walking unit. If they made an arrest they called it in on the pay phone and the white officers would come to their location and transport the poisoner to jail. These same white officers and supervisors were still working on the force when I joined.

My focus was my family and providing a good life for my kids.

These encounters as I look back on them did not affect me as much as what I have had to deal with, with my kids.

Part of the reason is because those incidents lasted a short period of time, where I have been dealing with my kid's attitudes for over twenty plus years.

As my career winded down, I survived, flourished and retired after thirty three years, as a police Lieutenant.

CHAPTER FIVE

JOSIE

Another Reason:

I am currently in a long term relationship that my kids have a hard time accepting. Her name is Josie and she is also 23 years younger than me which puts her around the age of my kids. The picture below is included for two reasons. One is to show that she is not African American and two, to show what attracted me to her, she is stunning.

As you can imagine they had a hard time adjusting to this relationship. Neither my second wife nor current girlfriend never tried to be a mother to my kids. In my opinion they both did everything to try to embrace them and make them feel wanted in our lives. I can't say the same for Josie kids toward me. That is a subject for another time.

She had four children when I met her, two boys and two girls. The only reason I will included them is because I truly thought that my kids were nothing like hers when it came to being respectful. I have always considered my kids to be respectful to me and others. Now I realize that although they are a part of me with many of my traits, they were not raised like me or by me.

Josie kids have shown a tremendous amount of disrespect to me over the past 20 years. They too were very young when I entered their lives. They have treated their mother the same way my kids have treated me. She left the marriage to get away from the abuse at the hands of her spouse and the kids because of their young age at the time didn't understand why she left. It's sad that they treat their step-dad better than their biological mother.

Just as with my kids, Josie children have no understanding of what sacrifices she has made in order for them to have the life they enjoy today. She is part Native American and lived on a reservation, in Washington State, until getting married to their dad. I have visited her tribe, Lummi Nations, on several occasions and I can say that it is as bad as the projects that I grew up in. Like most reservations, it has its share of drug and alcohol abuse, poverty and unemployment.

Most of her family is still there. She was fortunate to have been able to leave. Her kids have no idea what their life would have been like had she stayed.

Some of the things that they have said and done to me, is so bad that I refuse to address them in this book. I made it a point to never tell my kids what I was going through with Josie's kids, I didn't want them to get involved. All I can say is that I felt my kids would never act that way because they were raised better. To my surprise, they did.

Some of the words out of my two oldest mouth is worse than anything Josie kids have said to me.

Recently I traveled to Austin to visit my oldest and her new grandson, my first great grandson. My plan while I was there was to have a face to face talk with my son since we had argued over the phone weeks earlier.

Once I arrived in Austin at 10pm. I called my daughter and told her I was in town and wanted to visit the following day. The conversation turned confrontational quickly. As a result I ended up having to drive back home the same night arriving way after 2am. and tired. I did not get to see my great grandson and had to deal with my son the next day, after my daughter told him that I was in town to talk with him face to face. I guess he misinterpret what my intentions were, or she didn't communicate correctly what my intentions were. I wanted to make amends not go to war. He started texting me the next day and gave me what I felt was the ultimate disrespect, he addressed me in a text message, as DUDE, instead of dad. This gave a clearer picture of how easily he can be played. I didn't ask my daughter to tell him I was in town, I can only imagine that she wanted to involve him in order to feel and confirm to herself that I was the problem. If I was fighting with both of them then I have a problem, not her.

The following text message that day from my son was the last communication I had with him.

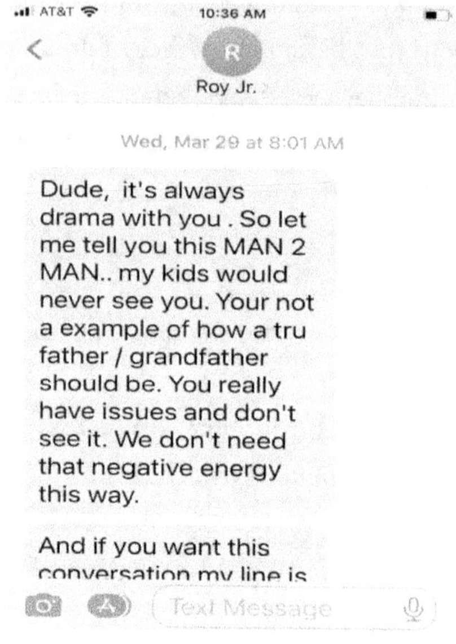

She did reach out the next day with two apologies via text which I didn't respond to. I expect my kids to be adult enough to pick up the phone and say, I'm sorry or pay a visit the way I attempted, if you are really sorry. Besides, the apologies are twenty years too late. The damage has been done and I'm not sure it can be fixed, it never hurts to try, and that's what I have been trying to do on my end all these years.

After so many years of trying to make up for the past which you can't do. I decided that maybe it's time to stop trying. I decided that I would not talk to them for a while and see if they realize and understood that at my age I don't have that many years guaranteed and each day wasted is a horrible mistake.

My current girlfriend went through this with her oldest daughter. The daughter didn't talk to her for three years. I couldn't imagine why a child would do this to their parent, only to find myself in the same situation.

These young adults who think they are smarter than their parents have no idea of what they are doing. They don't understand that they can't get back all the months and years thrown away. They act as if their parent will live forever.

They are in for an awaking when their kids start to treat them the same way, and it will happen, trust me.

My youngest daughter Tiff, really surprised me. She has struggled since her teenage years. She was the only one who didn't play sports and get a scholarship.

She is now working in Austin as a Nurse.

She joined the military and served in the Navy for two years before being injured and honorably discharged. My two other kids didn't serve. This may be the difference in how Tiffany shows the expected respect to her father and the other two don't. The military will teach you that if your parents fail to do so.

She had to raise two children as a single parent. She worked hard in spite of some medical issues. Her and I have a good relationship and she has said on several occasions that the problem I am having with my two other kids, is a result of what was fed to them early on. I think her for acknowledging that and most of all for overcoming it. I suspect she may face some criticism from her mom and siblings but I know that she can handle anything thrown her way, besides, the truth is the truth. It's nothing that I didn't already know for the past twenty years.

So I say to anyone living through a similar relationship, don't beat up on yourself. The kids have to become adults and figure it out for themselves. They have to look at the parent that's preaching evil about the other parent and understand why. I know it's hard when you are very young but once you become a teenager and young adult, you should question and correct those lies that were told to you.

Example:

This is still hard for me to swallow but recently while talking to my son, he told me a story of what happen to him as a kid. He said that his mom sent him from Austin to Corpus to stay with me because of his behavior. This was not the first time, I will address the other one.

He said that when he got to Corpus that I was not there to pick him up at the bus station.

His mom or him, never called me to tell me that he was coming. I didn't talk to her to begin with. She could have had him call as before and I would have had no problem picking him up in Corpus, I missed him and wanted to see him anytime.

I have no idea what transpired between him and her as far as someone not communication with me. I would hate to think that she intentional sent him here knowing that I wouldn't be there to pick him up. What's worse is why didn't he use a payphone at the bus station and call me to let me know he was in town. Even if he didn't know my number he should have gotten it before coming, he could have called my place of employment which is open 24 hours a day, the Police Department as ask them to contact me.

To be honest I question if this really happen base of the first time he came on a bus.

The first bus trip was when he was to arrive in Corpus at the bus station around midnight or later. I had just gotten off of work that night and was chilling in my hot tub, waiting on his call. The call came but instead of it being at Corpus bus station, he was still in San Antonio at the bus station.

To make a long story short, he missed his connect from San Antonio to Corpus for reasons unknown. When I arrived in San Antonio and found that his luggage was on the bus going to Corpus, we exchanged some words on the streets and he ran off. I was shocked because I had never seen this side of him and didn't expect it. I searched for a while and couldn't locate him, I left his ticket at the window for a return trip home. He got home safely and I missed out on another opportunity to spend quality time with him.

Again, as my mother and many parents tell their kids, if you don't have anything good to say, don't say anything.

As I said before I don't talk with their mother and haven't in over 40 years. Do I blame her, what do you think?

As in most divorces there is a lot more to the divorce that don't need to be mentioned in this book or anywhere else other than my memory and hers.

This has been the single most troubling experience in my life, second only to my sons passing.

CHAPTER SIX

FAMILY TREE

One of the reasons I wrote this book is because I don't know anything about my family on either my mothers or fathers side. There's not much that I wanted to know, if I did I would have asked my mom when she was alive. I don't recall my brother Fred asking many questions either. I don't know if it was growing up in the ghetto that harden us or if my mom prepared us, in her own way, she wanted us to be strong and survive.

As I reflect back on my mom I am amazed that I never heard my mom complain about anything. She faced ever challenges head on and there were many.

She never remarried but there were several men in our life. The odd thing was their names which at our age was somewhat embarrassing. The two were named, Mop and Mr. Lucky.

I don't know why we called him Mr. Lucky, I can only surmise that it was out of respect that we added the Mr. to his name when speaking of him.

Mop on the other hand got his name from the wig that he wore. It was shaped like a mop and I never saw him take it off.

Not once in either of my mom's relationships did Fred or I ever disrespect her boyfriends. The thought never crossed our minds. It wasn't that they were her partners but rather we had been raised to respect anyone our senior no matter what.

Anyway, I do sometime wonder about those grandparents and how they lived. At this point there is no family members that can fill in those blanks.

I am not as close to my grandkids as I would like. I recently tried reaching out to my son's daughter who recently graduated from college.

My son takes a lot of pride in raising his kids. Because of his recent behavior I don't know what to expect from him, if I tried contacting his kids, my grandkids.

I want to respect him as a father, I just wished that he would respect me as the grandfather and his father.

I have seen many grandparents go through situations like this with their kids, which is more common that most people realize. These grandparents go as far as taking their own kids to court in order to get permission to visit their grandkids. I would never think of doing such a thing.

I did text his daughter to say congratulations on her graduation from college. She did reply and said thank you. I tried again to call and talk with her but I never received a reply, so I dropped it. I didn't want to chance any more nasty messages from my son. I rather hold on to the good memories we had for many years, even if they were not sincere. I can't imagine how my kids could fake their feelings on all the visits I made to see them, for so many years.

As a police officer it's important to be able to read people, I guess I dropped the ball this time.

I only hope one day that they don't look back like I am and want to know about the relatives on my side of the family. There are few left standing.

I don't expect that my mom's or dad's side of the family will yield any doctors, lawyers or saints. I clearly understand the time that they lived in which presented few if any opportunities to have a good education or great life. I just wished that my kids had that same level of understanding, my life was nothing like theirs or their mothers. She came from a two parent household with a working dad, for many years.

One good example of what can happen when family don't keep in touch is what happen to me several years ago.

We had an uncle name Daisy Dukes who owned a good size piece of land in Luling, Texas. As kids we would visit and go horseback riding. He had oil on his land and my mom's brother and sisters would get a monthly check from the oil company for drilling on the land.

When he passed the land was handed down to a family member who failed to pay taxes on it for several years and as a result the land went to auction and was lost, oil well and all.

Having said that, my goal in life was to make something of myself that would make my mom and kids proud. I worked long and hard to accomplish that only to feel that it is unappreciated by my kids. My mom, when she was alive and I became a police officer was so proud that I can still see it in her smile. I am sure she felt a lot of pride in knowing that one of her three boys did good, there is no doubt that she loved all three of us the same, she never showed any favoritism or resentment toward any of us.

I served my country in the military, I served the city I lived in my whole life as a police officer of 33 years, I graduated from college as the first one in my family to do so, I became the first black police chief in South Texas. I became a private investigator and tried passing that off to my son. I own my own company and wrote my first book prior to this one.

But let it be told, I am such a bad parent because life happened.

Don't get me wrong, I am no saint. I am very stubborn which is why I didn't **try** drugs and alcohol. Very direct and opinionated and some would say somewhat mean.

My nickname at the police department was Sgt. Rock, I trained the police cadets for five years and I was intentionally hard, for their own survival once they got to the streets as police officers.

I have high expectations for myself and the people around me. I hate to hear excuses, just get it done.

With today's technology there is no excuse for ignorance, the world is at your fingertips.

Once you become an adult you can make yourself a better person.

I don't drink, never smoked. I have never done drugs or been arrested. I believe in God and live my life as a Christian.

The two beliefs I have always lives by is:

1. What goes around comes around.
2. Treat people fair and good things will come your way.

I sometimes feel like there's a guardian angel looking after me. I really shouldn't be here today. I have been shot, shot at, and hit by a train, battle cancer.

My mom raised us to be religious, I no longer attend church but the belief is still there.

I have no idea what my kids religious beliefs are. I assumed that they do or did attend church as children, at least I hope so. Over the years I have never had a religious conversation with any of them. When I look back I realize that part of the blame might lie with me for assuming that they were getting what they needed from their mom and her family. Their grandparents were very religious people when I knew them.

I am sure like so many people that they would swear that they are close to god, not understanding that if that is true then their actions, especially toward me for so many years, would reflect that. If I was the worst parent in the world, the bible talks about forgiveness. I don't see this in them.

I can truly say that I have forgiven them for all of the things that they have done to hurt me. They are a part of me and I only want the best for them and their kids, my grandkids.

They can continue to preach to anyone who listen about what a bad parent I am, if I am a bad parent then I must also be a bad person.

I think anyone looking at my life or any knowledge of me, would never call me a bad person.

I have touched so many people lives in my career as a police officer, in my everyday life, that on a consistent bases I have people that I don't even remember approaching me and telling me of how I had such a positive effect on their lives. This is hard to take when you have grown men and women telling you that you meant so much to them and you don't feel that you did anything special.

I will say that looking back I feel my true calling would have been teaching. I have always tried to teach people. Doing my years of playing and coaching basketball at the YMCA, training police officers to get prepared for a tough job on the streets or working with kids in numerous programs like D.A.R.E. and P.A.L. Police Athletic League.

I got the opportunity to give back again to my neighborhood. The Police Department received a Grant to help the people in the North Side of Corpus. They asked for a volunteer and I stepped up. I worked with a lot of kids, parents, trying to help them deal with the rough life in the projects.

What's sad is that today the entire community that I grew up in has been demolished to make way for a new bride and businesses. The people have been relocated throughout the city.

⸜⸍

Chapter Seven

End of Duty

After serving thirty three years as a Police Lieutenant with the Corpus Christi Police Department I retired in 2006, I spent a considerable amount of time going to Austin Texas to visit with my kids. Each visit would start off with a family dinner at a restaurant. This included my kids, their spouses and my grandkids. There was never an invite to their homes for a barbeque or family dinner, I did visit my daughters homes a few times but have never step foot in my son home. They would always meet at the restaurant or come by my hotel room.

It was understood by them that before I return home, I would empty my pockets of all the money I had left over, and give it to them. I had no problem doing this because I felt that they needed it.

I will say that I probably would have visited more often if I didn't feel the pressure to have lots of money to spend on them each trip. Some visits were for school clothes, new tires, computers and laptops and paying overdue bills.

Many times I questions whether they wanted to see me or just wanted money. I didn't really care, because I wanted to see them.

At no time on any of the visits, did any of my kids offer to pick up the tap for dinner, which was always a good amount. I never once asked them to do so. They have NEVER asked me if I need any financial assistance, which I haven't needed since leaving home at age 20 for the army.

I have not heard the words, dad, do you need anything, but instead I always heard, dad I need. I talking about their adult years.

Looking back this should have been a sign that they were not being taught the way I was raised. As you know it's the offer that counts, which never came. I would have never allowed them to pay.

The following years after I retired from the police department, I took several jobs, two as police chief in small departments. I got the opportunity to learn about small town politics.

Doing a time as police chief I learned that I was the first black police chief in South Texas. This gave me a lot of pride and I knew without a doubt that it would make my kids proud. To this day they have not acknowledged this achievements.

After leaving law enforcement I worked as a private investigator for a friend of mine. I wanted to see if I would like this type of work. It was very similar to what I did the past 33 years as a police officer but without all of the restrictions.

My friend didn't provide any training, he also had just retired from the same police department as I. He felt that with my background and many years of experience that I would figure it out, and I did.

I enjoyed it so much that I decided to have my own company. I applied with the Department of Public Safety for a license. I did all of the necessary things such as taking a written exam, background check and getting the required insurance.

I created my own website without any experience in this area and secured my own advertising.

Once I started my company I saw the opportunity to get my kids involved. This was going to be an opportunity of a life time for them.

They didn't have to test or be trained. I would provide the training myself. I started with my son who was not happy with his current job and constantly in need of additional funds to support his family and do all of the things that he was doing with the kids. Taking them to basketball camps, tournaments and things.

I explained to him because I was the owner of a company it would be easy for him to get a license. We got him one and I asked him to search for clients in the Austin area and I would be there to assist him, to my knowledge, he never did.

With no law enforcement experience I explained to him that I would teach him everything that he needed to know. That upon completion of his training he could possibly apply for a job in Austin making considerably more money than his current job.

He responded as if he was really interested. He had already majored in Criminal Justice and has his associate degree in that field.

I started making notes of things that he needed to know but as I attempted to start the training, he failed the show any type of commitment to learning the job. He didn't get the necessary tools to do the job and was not willing to complete the assignments.

This is the only time that I can truly say, I was disappointed with him. He may say otherwise but it is not true.

I saw this as an opportunity to involve all my kids in this high-paying profession, which may never come around for them again. They do not have the required experience in law enforcement to start such a business, if they work for another company they would only be paid minimum pay, nothing close to what they could make with my company.

During my police career I watched many of my friends give their kids opportunities that were available only because of the contacts that they had in the community or jobs they held, I wanted to do the same.

Since I started my business I have had many people that I didn't know reach out to me and wanted to get into this field.

This is such an exciting profession to work in, especially for those who wanted to get into law enforcement but came up short.

The training notes that I had taken down for several years was published in my first book, Private Investigator Guide. I had never given any thought to writing a book. This turned out to be one of my biggest achievements in life, being an Author.

If you are interested in learning about this field, I suggest you read my book. It is listed on Amazon and Barnes and Noble.

Again, my thinking was, this should make my kids proud. Well guess what, they have never shown the response that one would expect, dad I'm proud of you, or anything close.

At this point in my life I have concluded that no matter what I accomplished in life, I would never get any acknowledgment or respect from them, just complaints, with the exception of Tiff. My youngest daughter is the exception. She has always been there to support me.

I hope that one day my kids don't look back at this once-in-a-lifetime opportunity and regret not taking advantage of it. At this time I don't think they realize that it is an opportunity not only for them but their kids as well.

I am currently still working as a private investigator. I recently reached out to my youngest daughter and her daughter to get them involved. They to, have failed to reply. Sorry Tiff, honesty and fairness is everything.

I hope by the time I publish this book that someone in my family steps up, before I close my business.

Once my company is closed there will be no opportunity for any of the family to work in this profession.

After retiring from the police department I had no illusions that my kids would throw me a retirement party of any sort. I did think that they might at least take me to dinner or something.

This never happened, they didn't attend the retirement ceremony, ask about it or to see pictures. As a matter of fact I don't think they even knew that I retired. They never asked, dad, when are you going to retire? I guess they must have thought I was superman and would never get injured in such a stressful and dangerous job. I rather believe this than think that they just didn't care.

What's interesting is that they have never once asked about my work. Not about any calls that I made that were dangerous or any murder cases I worked on. I, like most police officers get these questions from friends and family on a regular bases.

So to all you parents out there, especially your dad's, who is busting your butts to make your kids proud, I hope that they are nothing like my kids. As I stated before I don't blame the kids for their actions. I just wish that they were wise enough and mentally strong enough to get past all of the misinformation that they were given.

CHAPTER EIGHT

∽

REPEATING HISTORY

I have talked a lot about how things got this way. Without pointing the finger at any one person in particular, I am very concern that the process is being repeated.

By this I mean that since I am somewhat isolated from my grandkids because of my fragile relationship with their parents. I can see them, my two oldest kids, repeating the same mistakes that were made with them. When I say parents I am talking about my kids only. They are now the parent and appear to not be trying to grow the relationship between their kids and me. I don't know what they tell their kids about me, why I don't see them much or talk to them on the phone. I don't know if they are teaching them to embrace me and my side of the family or not, I doubt it.

I hope and pray that they are not projecting their animosity toward me onto their kids. This will be the same mistake that their mom made. Just like her they will fail to see it now as a mistake and think that they are protecting them from who knows what. If so, I hope that one day, when they become smart adults that their kids don't look back and ask them why they said such bad things about a good person, a blood relative, their grandfather whose name will live on through them.

Now that I am on the subject I should have seen this coming a long time ago. I named my first son the same as me as most proud dads do. My son Roy Gardner Jr. I thought would name his son Roy Gardner III.

As I stated before I tried reaching out to my son's daughter unsuccessfully. I have had little interaction with his two boys. This was many years ago. They have now grown into young adults. I don't have any way of contacting them.

My oldest daughter who recently became a grandmother is also sheltering of her kids. I have somewhat of a relationship with her oldest daughter. I have not had much interaction with her youngest daughter in years. They are both really good kids and independent in their thinking. I can see having a better relationship with them in the future than with my son's children.

I am intentionally not mentioning them by name for privacy reasons.

As I stated before I have not seen my great-grandson.

I have a better relationship with the grandkids of my youngest daughter.

In the years to come I would not be surprise if my grandkids express the same feelings for me as my kids.

As I stated before my kids are not close to each other the way they should be, therefore they are not teaching their kids to embrace their family outside of their home.

Over the 20 plus years I have never been to a reunion or barbeque in Austin where all three of my kids and their kids was present. They have not traveled together to my knowledge or planned a family reunion, or even attend church together.

This is not the dynamics I envisioned as a dad when I wanted kids. I remember the things that Fred and I did together and I always wished I would have had a sister.

One of the main reasons that I am writing this book is so my grandkids, should they ever want to know the truth about me, can read it for themselves.

After the recent problems with my two oldest, I wanted to reach out to my grandkids but like with my kids mother I didn't want to deal with the ongoing drama with the grandkids parents and put them in the middle by demanding to be part of their lives.

I don't think my kids see what they are doing or maybe they are so filled with bitterness that they don't care.

I use the word bitterness because who would keep their kids from seeing their grandparent?

I am aware that they have a relationship with the other grandparent as they should.

As far as my situation is concerned, only time will tell and I don't have that much time to waste.

I have recently as I got older, started to have some medical issues. Needless to say I have gotten no assistance from my kids.

I had two full knee replacements in 2022, I battled cancer from 2016-2022. Two eye surgeries.

My son indicated that he would come down for the knee surgery if I needed him and I felt really good about the offer. I didn't take him up on it because of his recent words and actions toward my girlfriend. And this was before he went ballistic with his last text messages. I didn't want or need any distractions at that time, so I declined his offer.

I felt that if he really was concerned about me and my recovery, he would have come anyway or at least followed up after the surgery.

He has express his dislike for my girlfriend for a long time. A big part of how he feels is based on money. He is concerned that should something happen to me, then she would benefit instead of him and the other kids.

This is not a concern of mine for several reasons. In spite of the recent medical procedures I am still in great shape. This comes from exercising my entire life.

I go to the gym several days a week, ride my bicycle several days and shoot pool all day every day. This is my therapy to deal with all the noise in my life.

Another stress reliever is my 2008 Hog, Fat Boy motorcycle. I don't ride it that much because of the distracted drivers on the road.

Another reason is that my girlfriend does not have access to my finances. I do plan to assist her as much as possible should we break up or something happens to me. I feel that after 20 years of living with me, she deserves nothing less, regardless of how my kids feel. They are not here taking care of me on a daily bases, actually not at all. She may not be the best provider and brings a lot of drama, but she is here.

The reason I knew my son was not as concern about my health and more concern about my finances is because, he has talked for years about wanting me to give him Power Of Attorney over me. I laughed the first time he said it, I thought he was joking. I am as sharp today as I was 40 years ago. I challenge myself both mentally and physically on a regular bases.

I just talked about my weekly exercise regiment, which is amazing for a 70 something year old person.

When I go to the gym, I go strong, always have and always will, no matter how much pain I might be feeling. I don't do pain medication at all, (no pain no gain).

He went so far as to say that he had already drawn up the papers. I knew this was not the case. This is the same person who wouldn't apply himself for different jobs I sent his way, including the PI job.

Why would someone even think of doing something like that before a person is either on their sick bed, or me asking him to do it?

I guess he has not heard about what's called a Will. If I was that concerned about my estate I would have one, everyone should.

After reading this far about my relationship with my family, would you be concerned about leaving your life saving to them? I will have to think long and hard about what I want to do about this.

Blood is thicker than water but water keeps you alive.

Our last conversation before things went sour was him telling me that he was parked in a pawnshop parking lot getting ready to sell his gun. I question why he even had a gun collection, watch collection, car collection, and cigar collection and not able to pay his bills. I have had to assist him for years financially. He tries to do so much for his kids and show them what a real dad does as oppose to his dad who was not there for him, that he appears to be living beyond his means.

What was surprising to me was to find out that I don't really know my son the way I thought I did. He appears to have tunnel vision about a lot of things around him, and lacking empathy.

He fails to understand the concept of divorce and how common it is when two people can't get alone. He is fortunate enough to be in a relationship where he is in the home with his kids. This should be a blessing for him and not a comparison to me.

I hope that none of his kids ever treat and talk to him the way he has done to me.

I went to some of his daughter's basketball games when she was in high school and was somewhat embarrassed for her, the way he acted. You know what I am talking about. The parent or ex-jock who think that they know better than the coach on how the team should play. I don't know if he continues this approach with his younger sons, I hope not.

I know his intentions are sincere but like a lot of ex-players, they try to relive his glory days through his kids.

I think this authoritarian approach on the court has carried over to his family life, and could bring unexpected results for him from his kids, later in life. I don't know if being 6 feet 8 inches tall, has him thinking that he is king. I know I use to think I was invincible when I reached a certain fitness level, and I am only six feet two. It took a broken jaw to bring me back to earth.

With no disrespect I will go out on a limb and say that my son is not a warrior. I have never heard of him being in a fight with anybody. I think this is a good thing, because it means that he never had to experience the things that I experience in life.

Example- one day I decided to skip school and hang out with a person I thought was cool. He was a little older and bigger and I don't remember what grade I was in. We walked around looking to get into trouble and he asked me if I had any money. I replied yes, fifty cents. He said, give it to me and I responded I'm not. He made a fist and struck me in the stomach knocking the wind out of me, I was barely able to get the money out quick enough before being hit again. Needless to say, I never skipped school again.

But what really got me with my son, was some words that I will not repeat, that came out of his mouth. I was in awe that my son would say such things. One comment was about my son Zane, who is deceased and the other was in a text message about my current girlfriend Josie.

This occurred in May or June of 2023 and he has yet to apologize. I think he feels that what he said was justified. He failed to think about how he would feel if I said the same about his spouse. I would never think of doing anything like that, my MOTHER, taught me better.

I never thought a child of mine would be so cold. I have never with good reasons, spoke that way to him or my girls about their mother, it would be justified.

Looking back I sometimes wish that I had protected them from the collateral damage of the divorce. Instead of in the trenches, face to face with her, I could have used the courts and asked for joint custody.

I remember at the time of the separation I asked them if they wanted to live with me or their mother, they chose their mother, which I agreed to without a fight. They didn't like some of the strict rules that I had and knew that they would enjoy a lot of freedom living with her.

I doubt if they recall this conversation and when they read this like most of the book they will say that these things didn't happen.

As I sit here I find that a lot of this chapter is about my son and not the girls. The reason is that I though he and I was in a good place for many years. Now that I see that he was pretending, it hurts more.

As I said before my youngest daughter and I are in a good place. She understands me the most and know that no matter what I do, don't do or say, it doesn't take away from how I feel about my kids.

I feel the same way now about my grandkids and great grandson. I don't have to see them all the time or talk to them. I have too many to even try to remember their birthdays or other important dates. As long as I know that they are in a good place, I am happy. I may never see my great-grandsons but he is always in my heart.

I remember my oldest daughter telling me before I arrived on the long trip to visit him, dad, watch what you say, I couldn't believe my daughter was lecturing me on what to say.

She, on the other hand don't pull any punches. I have known how she felt about the divorce from day one. Most times she manages to keep her feelings under control. But I can always see it in her eyes and body language.

The last conversation we had, prior to this book, she unleashed it on me. This was the night I drove there to see my great grandson. Over the phone she laid down the law and told me that if I didn't comply then I wasn't welcomed, not in those exact words. This was the night at 1am. I had to turn around and drive another four hours home, instead of her giving me shelter for the night.

I am proud to say that in many ways she has many of my traits. She is a very hard worker and is focused on her goals in life. She and her family appears to be having a good life and I hope it continues for ever.

She speaks her mind but fail to understand that there is a line when it comes to her parents.

She has accomplished a lot in her life. She has two beautiful daughters, a grandson, which I haven't seen and a hard working husband, who is more respectful to me than my own kids.

It's obvious that he had a good upbringing. I would like to shout out to his family for having such a respectful, hardworking man in their family. I have never met any of his family but if they are anything like him then they are good people.

Chapter Nine

I Surrender

At this point in my life I have decided to stop trying to make up for something I didn't do and can't fix. I feel I have done my very best to be the father I should be. The same way I tried to be the best husband and father when my family was still whole.

I have been there whenever they needed me. And there were many times that they needed me. I spent most of my life going to see them and now that I have gotten older it should be the other way around, but it's not.

My kids especially my son probably regret that their dad wasn't there to play sports with them or do homework, etc. I don't think that they realize that every time I see the neighbors son coming over to help his dad with the yard, or dads and their kids eating at a restaurant, playing pool together, etc., I think about my kids not being in my life now, the way they accuse me of not being in theirs then.

The only difference is that I can't find a good reason for them not being here, I had what I thought was a necessary one. One that was to protect them from a dysfunctional marriage, filled with daily arguments and physical altercations, with me being on the receiving end. What's theirs? Holding on to lies that were told to them by a vindictive, jealous person who wanted to hurt me. But since I was no longer in the house, the plan was to attack me verbally through my kids, which ended up hurting them more.

I don't know how long before I talk to my two oldest again or their kids. I talk to Tiffany on a regular bases and occasional her kids. I want her to know that in this book, when I refer to 'My Kids', I am not talking about her, we have a great relationship and always will. I think that her struggles in life and military experience is very similar to what I have encountered in life and it makes us stronger. This is not to say that my two oldest have not dealt with adversity but not to the same degree as Tiff.

I have no plans to reach out to them anytime soon,

I feel that it's time that they step up and grow up, to except the facts that they was misled, brainwashed, and used. Which resulted in them being disrespectful, cold and rude toward their father.

With today's technology separated parents are able to communicate with their kids at almost any age. Kids are given cell phones and computers and well equipped on how to use them. Some parents use tracking devices that are hidden in the kids backpack or clothing as a means of knowing where the kids are at any given time.

The courts are more involved in these case than when I went through this. It is a lot easier to get full or joint custody today.

After saying this, I as a private investigator and ex-police officer still see these vindictive parents who use their kids in order to punish the other spouse. They have no idea of the amount of collateral damage that they are doing to the kids.

Almost half of the cases I work as a PI has to do with child custody. Parents spend a considerable amount of time and money looking for dirt on the other parent as oppose to bringing the family closer together, even though they are separated or divorced.

I spoke earlier about my mom spanking us with a tree branch. I do not recall ever spanking my kids when they lived under my roof or after. It makes me question what might had been difference if we as parents weren't so lenient back then. I have no regrets on how I disciplined them.

It wasn't the lack of discipline that got us here, but the lack of leadership, good parenting and many other factors that went on in their home after the divorce. I also share some of the blame for decisions I made after the divorce.

One fact has materialized from this tragedy, is that words hurt more than physical pain. The words they were told have lasted for over 40 years and counting. The two oldest have become angry and distant from me. Many times they try not to show it but it's always there.

I hope and pray that someday they can really get past these lies and realize what a waste of time has occurred on both sides.

I have always wondered if my kids have ever held the person responsible for this travesty, accountable. If so, they have never spoke to me about it. At this stage in life I think it's probably too late to even consider, the damage has already been done and in my observation, it's unrepairable.

The war is over, I raise the white flag and surrender. God Bless us all. They have my number and know where I live.

In the event that we are back communicating before this book is published, I have no regrets about anything that is said in the book. I am actually hoping that once they read the book they will have a different perspective on our relationship. I don't really believe this because of all the built-up anger for so many years, but I am willing to hope, what other choice do I have?

I just hope that they realize that my intentions were not to attack their mother, them or their character but to express what I have had to live through for the past 40 years, and to one day have a relation-ship with my grandkids and great grandkids.

If I offend anyone, especially my kids, I sincerely apologize.

To my readers, both men and women, don't be the parent that sabotages the relationship between your kids and the other parent, take the high road. To those of you who may not yet be parents, don't make this mistake, you can't undo it. And to the kids who are the ones who have suffered the most, try to understand both sides before you past judgement. My kids never stop to ask me why, they just went with what they were told.

It's hard for me to understand that as parents themselves, they don't respect me the way they expect their kids to respect them. I feel sure that if they or their spouses went to prison, the way my brother did, or got divorce, they would still expect their kids to respect them.

You would think with all of the crazy things going on in this world today, they would have a different perspective on life.

We all will have to answer to a higher power someday. So, if you feel that you did your best and your intentions were good, live with it, I have.

PEACE!